THIS LAND CALLED AMERICA: ALASKA

CREATIVE EDUCATION

Published by Creative Education
P.O. Box 227, Mankato, Minnesota 56002
Creative Education is an imprint of The Creative Company
www.thecreativecompany.us

Book and cover design by Blue Design (www.bluedes.com)
Art direction by Rita Marshall
Printed in the United States of America

Photographs by Alamy (Stephen Matera), Corbis (Brooklyn Museum, Momatiuk–Eastcott, Douglas Peebles, Richard Hamilton Smith, Paul A. Souders, Tim Thompson), Getty Images (Brett Baunton, Evans, General Photographic Agency, Henry Georgi, Fred Hirschmann, Ralph Lee Hopkins, Hulton Collection, Karen Kasmauski/National Geographic, DMITRI KESSEL, Randy Lincks, Harvey Lloyd, Arnaldo Magnani, Paul Souders, Bob Stefko, Tom Walker)

Library of Congress Cataloging-in-Publication Data
Peterson, Sheryl.
Alaska / by Sheryl Peterson.
p. cm. — (This land called America)
Includes bibliographical references and index.
ISBN 978-1-58341-627-3
1. Alaska—Juvenile literature. I. Title. II. Series.
F904.3.P44 2008
979.8—dc22   2007005679

First Edition
9 8 7 6 5 4 3 2 1

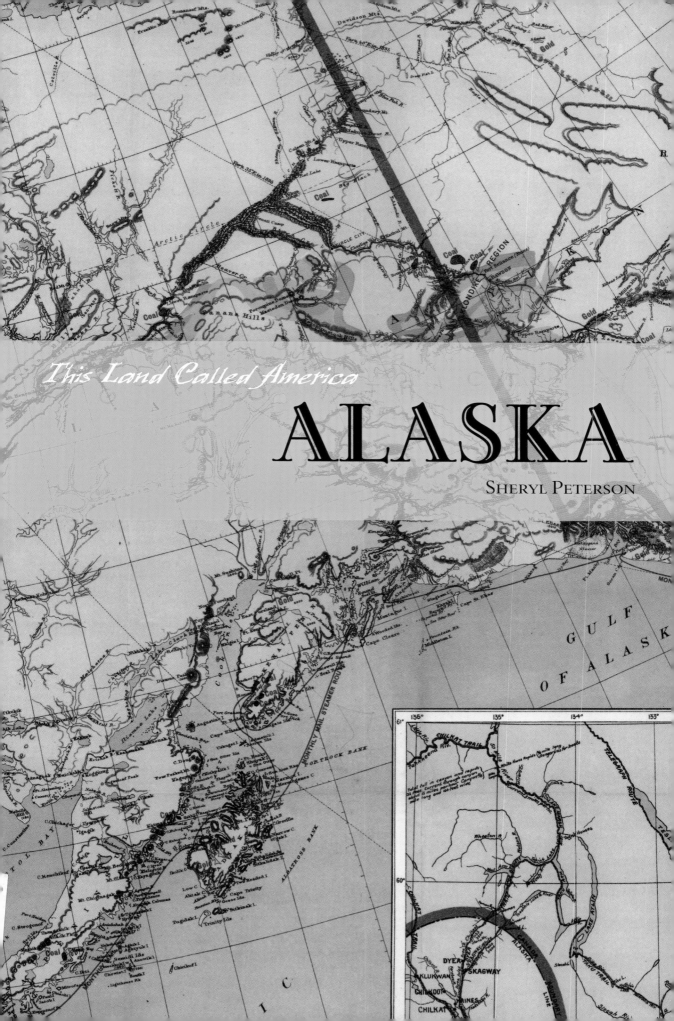

This Land Called America

ALASKA

Sheryl Peterson

Alaska

SHERYL PETERSON

IN ANCHORAGE, ALASKA, HUNDREDS OF DOGS STRAIN AGAINST THEIR HARNESSES. THEY YELP AND JUMP. DOG-SLED DRIVERS, OR MUSHERS, RECHECK THEIR GEAR. THEY POSE FOR PICTURES AND SIGN AUTOGRAPHS. THE "LAST GREAT RACE ON EARTH" IS ABOUT TO BEGIN. TEAMS CROSS FROZEN RIVERS AND JOURNEY OVER DANGEROUS MOUNTAIN TERRAIN. THEY MUSH ON THROUGH BLINDING BLIZZARDS. THE BRAVE DRIVERS AND DOGS ARE COLD AND TIRED BY THE TIME THEY CROSS THE FINISH LINE IN FARAWAY NOME. THESE FEARLESS DOG-SLED TEAMS CELEBRATE ALASKA'S GREAT FRONTIER PAST. THE CHALLENGING IDITAROD RACE IS A SYMBOL OF ALASKA, THE STATE WHERE EXCITING ADVENTURES AWAIT.

YEAR

1741 Danish-born explorer Vitus Bering and German scientist George Steller claim Alaska for Russia.

EVENT

More Than a Frozen Land

Millions of years ago, Alaska was connected to what is now Russia by a land bridge. Over time, the Bering Sea washed over the land. Eskimos, Aleuts, and American Indians moved into the area almost 2,000 years ago. Alaska's first European explorers came from Russia hundreds of years later.

Vitus Bering was a navigator in the Russian navy. He sailed east and first sighted the southern coast of Alaska in 1741. After that, some Russians settled in Alaska. They trapped sea otters and brought the furs back to Russia. A few Russian families settled in Alaska. Spaniards also explored the rugged coastline in the 18th century.

For a long time, people thought Alaska was too cold and too far away to inhabit. But in the mid-1800s, American fishing companies became interested. There were plenty of salmon and halibut in the waters off Alaska's coast. Fish canneries opened in the southern towns of Sitka and Klawock.

In the coastal town of Barrow, where most native Eskimos live (above), there are no mountains like those in Denali National Park (opposite).

YEAR
1778 Captain James Cook of England charts Alaska's coastline.
EVENT

The towns that sprang up during gold rushes in Alaska often started out as rows of tents along dirt roads.

In 1867, the United States bought Alaska from Russia. Andrew Johnson was the U.S. president at the time. His secretary of state, William Seward, paid $7.2 million for Alaska. Many people thought he paid too much and called the purchase "Seward's Folly." Some even referred to Alaska as "President Johnson's Polar Bear Garden."

Soon, people realized that Alaska was a wonderful place with forests, wildlife, and water resources. More fish canneries and sawmills popped up in southeastern Alaska. In 1880, a miner named Joseph Juneau found gold in southeastern Alaska and named the spot Juneau.

In 1898, men discovered gold near Nome on the southeastern Seward Peninsula in western Alaska. Four years later, miners uncovered gold nuggets in Pedro Creek and started the city of Fairbanks. Prospectors, or people looking for gold, rushed in by the thousands. By 1910, Alaska's population had almost doubled. Some people got rich, but many didn't. Food and supplies were very expensive. Eggs sometimes cost $20 a dozen!

The Alaska Territory was created by the U.S. Congress in 1912. By now, Alaska was more well-known and easier to access. A telegraph connected Alaska with the rest of the U.S., and a railroad was built from Seward to Fairbanks. In 1924, Alaska residents were finally able to receive mail. It came by air. Carl

A bush airplane can be fitted with tires, skis, or floats to help it land in any environment.

Ben Eielson was one of the first bush pilots to deliver mail to the remote region.

In 1943, while Franklin Roosevelt was president, the U.S. completed the Alaska Highway. The road joined Alaska with the "Lower 48," as the states were called. Army and Air Force bases were built in Alaska, and American soldiers were stationed there. They helped defend Alaska against the Japanese military during World War II. Finally, in 1959, Alaska became a state, with Juneau named state capital.

On March 27, 1964, a powerful earthquake shook Alaska. It was called "The Good Friday Earthquake." Buildings toppled, and cars and houses fell into giant cracks in the ground. A huge tidal wave swept over and damaged the coastal town of Valdez.

In 1968, the largest oil field in the U.S. was discovered at Prudhoe Bay, Alaska, near the Arctic Ocean. About 10 years later, the Trans-Alaska Pipeline was built to transport the oil. The pipeline was 800 miles (1,288 km) long. Alaska oil was so valuable that it was often called "black gold."

YEAR

1896   Gold is discovered in a stream off of the Klondike River in the Yukon.

EVENT

The Last Frontier

ALASKA IS ONE OF ONLY TWO U.S. STATES THAT ARE
NOT BORDERED BY ANOTHER STATE (HAWAII BEING THE
OTHER). ALASKA IS LOCATED AT THE NORTHWESTERN
TIP OF NORTH AMERICA. THE ARCTIC OCEAN SERVES AS
ITS NORTHERN BORDER. THE GULF OF ALASKA AND THE
NORTH PACIFIC OCEAN ARE TO THE SOUTH. CANADA IS
ALASKA'S NEIGHBOR TO THE EAST. THE BERING SEA AND
THE CHUKCHI SEA LIE BETWEEN ALASKA AND RUSSIA.

The name Alaska comes from the native Aleut word *alyeska,* which means "great land." Alaska is the largest state in America. It is twice as big as Texas, the second largest. Alaska also has the longest coastline. More than 1,800 islands, including the Aleutian Islands, lie along the 33,904-mile (54,563 km) Alaskan coast. Kodiak Island is the largest.

Majestic snow-topped mountains tower over the state. Part of the Rocky Mountain range runs across northern

Alaskan natives have always relied heavily on the sea to provide them with fish and other animals for food.

Anchorage (opposite), the site of a major gold rush, is the largest city in the "great land" of Alaska.

YEAR

1935   The U.S. offers inexpensive farmland in Alaska to Americans.

EVENT

- 13 -

Mount McKinley (opposite), originally called Denali ("The High One") by Indians, was renamed in 1896.

State bird: willow ptarmigan

Alaska. The Pacific Mountain System curves across southern Alaska and includes the Wrangell, Saint Elias, Alaska, and Coastal ranges. Mount McKinley is in the Alaska Range. Its peak rises 20,320 feet (6,194 m) above sea level and is the highest point in North America. Giant, slow-moving sheets of ice called glaciers lie at the foot of these mountains. Alaska is one of the few places in the world where it is still cold enough for larger glaciers to exist.

Between Alaska's mountain ranges are areas of rolling hills and muskeg. Muskeg is a soft, spongy type of soil. Along the Arctic Ocean, the land is much different. The arctic tundra is treeless land where the ground is always partially frozen. In the short summer season, the tundra is filled with wild irises and forget-me-nots, the state flower.

At Kenai Fjords National Park, people can walk up to active glaciers such as Exit Glacier (above).

YEAR

1942 Construction on the Alaska Highway, linking Fairbanks to British Columbia, begins.

EVENT

- *15* -

Alaska has more than 3,000,000 lakes and about 3,000 rivers. The Yukon is Alaska's longest river and is more than 1,400 miles (2,253 km) long. The Yukon River runs east to west and almost divides the state in half.

Alaska has a wealth of wildlife. There are more bald eagles in Alaska than in any other state. The eagles swoop down to pluck salmon out of lakes and rivers. Whales, seals, and otters swim along the coast. Caribou and brown bears tromp through the wilderness. Polar bears swim off the Arctic Ocean coastline.

Because Alaska is such a vast state, the weather varies greatly. Parts of Alaska receive up to 200 inches (508 cm) of snow and rain each year. During northern Alaska winters, there is very little daylight. In the town of Barrow in the far north, people live in darkness from mid-November through mid-January. In the summer, though, Alaskans have daylight almost 24 hours a day. In the city of Anchorage, it is possible to read a book outside at midnight!

To travel long distances
and find more food,
polar bears leap from
one piece of floating ice
to another.

Alaska has been called North America's last frontier. Alaska
still has large areas of wilderness with no houses, stores, or
people. Even getting into the state's capital, Juneau, is difficult.
The only way to reach the city is by boat or plane. Many
Alaskans want their land to stay undeveloped. Other people
hope to drill for more oil or log more trees. Nature is protected
in Alaska's 15 national parks and 16 wildlife refuges.

Greatland People

ALASKA HAS A LOT OF ROOM BUT NOT MANY PEOPLE. THERE IS ENOUGH SPACE FOR EVERY ALASKAN TO HAVE ONE SQUARE MILE (2.6 SQ KM) OF LAND TO HIM- OR HERSELF. IN FACT, THERE ARE MORE CARIBOU IN ALASKA THAN THERE ARE PEOPLE.

Today, Alaska is one of the fastest-growing states in America, but it still has the third-smallest population among the states. Only one-third of Alaskans were born there. Most residents live in or near the cities of Anchorage and Fairbanks.

About three-fourths of Alaskans have European back-grounds. After the Russians came to Alaska, so did the Irish, English, and Germans. Alaska also has a high population of Aleuts and Eskimos. Aleuts live on the Alaskan Peninsula and the Aleutian Islands. About 44,000 Eskimos live in Alaska. The Inupiat Eskimos live in the north. The Yupik live in the south. Many fish and raise reindeer for a living.

Children compete in tug of war on St. Paul Island, which has the largest Aleut community in the U.S.

There are so many caribou in Alaska that they can easily wander into a town and hold up traffic.

YEAR

1959   Alaska becomes the 49th state in the union on January 3.

EVENT

- *19* -

From mid-June to late August, the short Alaskan salmon season keeps fishermen and canneries busy.

People who live in the iciest and loneliest parts of Alaska must dress warmly and be able to find food.

There are many Eskimo villages in the snow-covered Alaskan Arctic. Most Eskimos live in Barrow, the northernmost town in the U.S. Alaskans in the Arctic used to use dog sleds for transportation. There are still some places in Alaska that can be reached only by dog sleds. Speedy snowmobiles can access the rest.

The first settlers in Alaska worked as miners, loggers, or fishermen. Alaskans today do those jobs and many others. Mining is Alaska's biggest business and brings in about 32 percent of Alaska's income. People in Fair-banks and Nome still mine for gold. There are also

1964 The largest earthquake ever to hit North America shakes southern Alaska on March 27.
EVENT

Since opening in 1977, the Trans-Alaska Pipeline has moved more than 15 billion barrels of oil.

zinc mines in northwestern Alaska, but oil mining is the state's biggest moneymaker. The Alaskan government earns billions of dollars from oil. Every year, each Alaskan receives about $1,000 in oil money from the state.

Other Alaskans fish for a living. There are plenty of salmon, halibut, and king crab to be had. Fishing companies ship tasty Alaska salmon all across America. Alaska does not have many farms, but in the Matanuska Valley, near Anchorage, farmers grow cabbages, potatoes, and oats in the long, sunlit summers. Others raise dairy cattle and chickens.

Many Alaskans work for the U.S. government in the national parks and forests. Others make a living in the tourism business. More than one million tourists visit Alaska each year. Massive cruise ships tour along the coast. Visitors can stand on

Glacier Bay National Park, near Gustavus, is a popular destination for Alaskan cruises.

YEAR

1968 The largest oil field on U.S. soil is discovered at Prudhoe Bay, Alaska.

EVENT

the decks in the crisp air and gaze at the magnificent scenery. They hope to see glaciers and lots of Alaskan wildlife—such as whales, seals, and caribou—on their trips.

Alaskans stay active with vigorous pastimes such as dog sledding. Libby Riddles was the first woman to win the Iditarod Trail Sled Dog Race in 1985. Another famous Alaskan dog sledder was Susan Butcher. Butcher was the first person to drive a dog-sled team to the top of Mount McKinley. Butcher won the Iditarod three years in a row from 1986 to 1988. She won again in 1990.

Another well-known Alaskan was Benny Benson. In 1926, the 13-year-old Benson won a student flag-designing contest. His design using the North Star and the Big Dipper was chosen by the territorial government to decorate the Alaskan flag. Benson received a gold watch and $1,000. Today, there is a memorial to Benson along the Seward Highway near the entrance to the city of Seward.

A statue of the Alaskan sled dog Balto was placed in New York City's Central Park in 1925.

Land of Adventure

In January 1925, children in the city of Nome became sick. They had a disease called diphtheria and needed a special serum, or medicine, to get well. The weather was extremely cold and snowy, but sled dogs and their mushers saved the day. The teams traveled more than 674 miles (1,085 km) from the railroad station in Nenana to Nome carrying

Training dogs to run races is a full-time job and begins at least one year before a race.

1973   The first Iditarod Trail Sled Dog Race is run from Anchorage to Nome.

the precious serum. The lead dog on the famous run was named Balto.

Dog sledding is now Alaska's state sport. To commemorate the run of 1925, musher Joe Redington Sr. began the Iditarod Trail Sled Dog Race in 1973. The big race covers 1,151 miles (1,852 km) as mushers travel from Anchorage to Nome. The race can last anywhere from 10 to 20 days. The weather is usually very cold as dogs and drivers cross the frozen lakes and rivers. Many volunteers help the participants get what they need and keep them safe.

Alaskans love their sports, but there are no professional teams in the state. The University of Alaska Seawolves thrill fans in Anchorage. Student athletes compete in Nordic skiing, basketball, track, and many other sports. The University of Fairbanks' Nanooks also host a variety of competitions. "Nanook" is the Eskimo word for polar bear.

Visitors can watch real bears in Denali National Park and Preserve. The scenic park has nearly six million acres (2.4 million ha) of land and is located about 240 miles (386 km) north of Anchorage. People go to Denali to see Alaska's "big five": moose, caribou, wolves, Dall sheep, and grizzlies. Visitors watch moose munching grasses and caribou resting on snowy patches. They spy curly-horned Dall sheep on the

There are plenty of places to ski in Alaska, including Ruth Glacier (above), in Denali National Park.

YEAR

1977

EVENT

The Trans-Alaska Pipeline, running north and south for 800 miles (1,288 km), begins operation.

Tufted puffins breed during the summer months on certain islands in Glacier Bay Park.

hillsides. Wolves sometimes trot by, and grizzly bears might be seen eating blueberries. Denali Park has a spectacular view of Mount McKinley's high, snowy peaks overhead.

Another adventure in Alaska is glacier viewing. There are about 100,000 glaciers in Alaska. Glacier Bay Park is a good place to see glaciers. Since there are no roads into the park, people must come by air or water. Hundreds of visitors arrive on cruise ships to watch the glaciers calve, or break off, into chunks of ice called icebergs.

Aurora borealises can take many forms and look like a curtain, band, arc, or patch of light.

YEAR
1989 The *Exxon-Valdez*, an oil supertanker, spills 11 million gallons (42 million l) of oil into Prince William Sound.
EVENT

- 28 -

Some people paddle sea kayaks among the icebergs and watch seals pop up in the water beside them. Orca and humpback whales also feed in Glacier Bay, making whale watching another popular pastime. Rare birds such as tufted puffins, arctic terns, and black oystercatchers are also found in Glacier Bay Park.

One of the most fascinating sights in the world occurs on dark nights in Alaska. Hardy Alaskans put on parkas and watch the sky from the tops of snow banks. The aurora borealis, or "northern lights," swirl and dance in dazzling ribbons of

In North America, brown bears are commonly called grizzly bears and grow into huge animals.

QUICK FACTS

Population: 663,661

Largest city: Anchorage (pop. 275,043)

Capital: Juneau

Entered the union: January 3, 1959

Nicknames: Last Frontier, Land of the Midnight Sun

State flower: forget-me-not

State bird: willow ptarmigan

Size: 663,267 sq mi (1,717,854 sq km)—biggest in U.S.

Major industries: fishing, tourism, oil and gas production, mineral mining

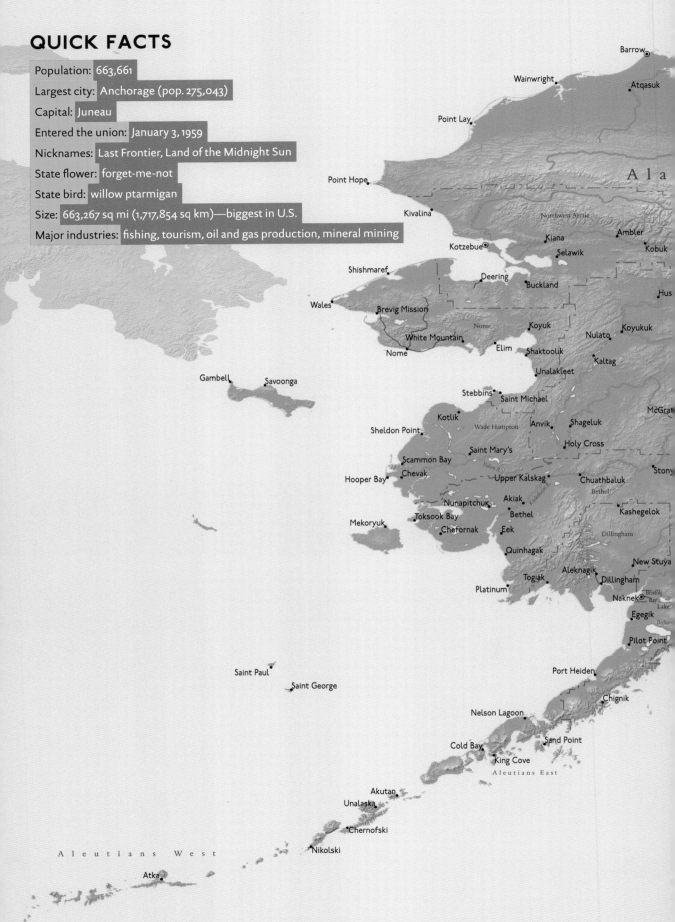

A l a

Barrow

Wainwright

Atqasuk

Point Lay

Point Hope

Kivalina

Northwest Arctic

Kiana

Ambler

Kobuk

Kotzebue

Selawik

Shishmaref

Deering

Buckland

Hus

Wales

Brevig Mission

Nome

Koyuk

Nulato

Koyukuk

White Mountain

Elim

Shaktoolik

Kaltag

Nome

Unalakleet

Gambell

Savoonga

Stebbins

Saint Michael

McGra

Kotlik

Anvik

Shageluk

Sheldon Point

Wade Hampton

Saint Mary's

Holy Cross

Scammon Bay

Yukon R.

Chuathbaluk

Stony

Hooper Bay

Chevak

Upper Kalskag

Bethel

Akiak

Nunapitchuk

Bethel

Kashegelok

Mekoryuk

Toksook Bay

Chefornak

Eek

Dillingham

Quinhagak

New Stuya

Aleknagik

Togiak

Dillingham

Platinum

Naknek

Bristol Bay

Egegik

Becharo

Pilot Point

Saint Paul

Port Heiden

Saint George

Chignik

Nelson Lagoon

Cold Bay

Sand Point

King Cove

Aleutians East

Akutan

Unalaska

Chernofski

A l e u t i a n s   W e s t

Nikolski

Atka

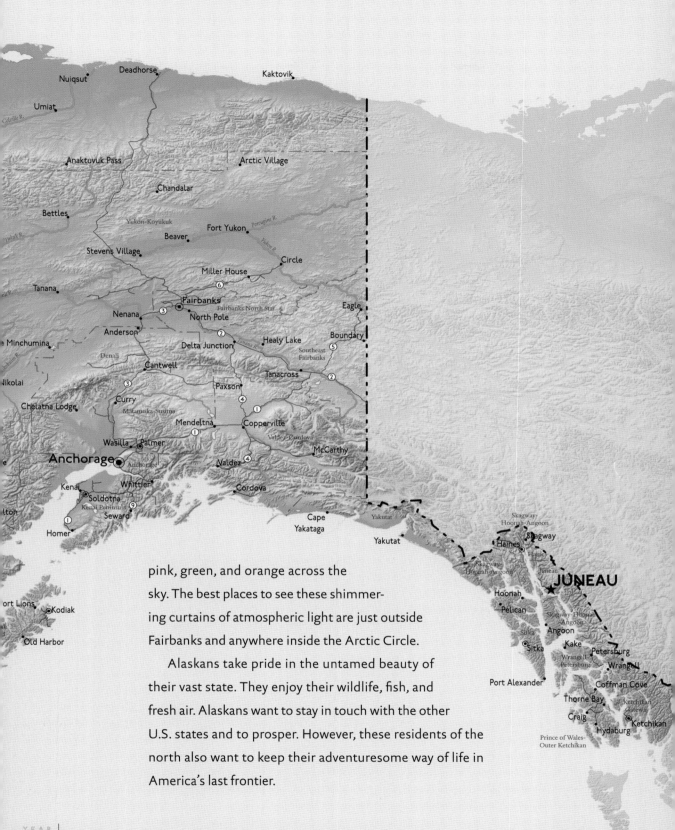

pink, green, and orange across the
sky. The best places to see these shimmer-
ing curtains of atmospheric light are just outside
Fairbanks and anywhere inside the Arctic Circle.

Alaskans take pride in the untamed beauty of
their vast state. They enjoy their wildlife, fish, and
fresh air. Alaskans want to stay in touch with the other
U.S. states and to prosper. However, these residents of the
north also want to keep their adventuresome way of life in
America's last frontier.

YEAR

2007   Lifelong resident Sarah Palin is sworn in as the first female governor of Alaska.

EVENT

BIBLIOGRAPHY

Alaska Travel Industry. "Explore Alaska." Alaska Travel Industry. http://travelalaska.com/Regions/StateRegions.aspx.

Fradin, Dennis B. *Alaska*. Chicago: Children's Press, 1977.

Gold Rush Centennial Task Force. "Gold Rush Stories." Gold Rush Centennial Task Force. http://www.library.state.ak.us/goldrush/STORIES?Timeline.htm.

Kummer, Patricia. *Alaska*. Mankato, Minn.: Bridgestone Books, 1998.

Marsh, Carole, and Kathy Zimmer. *Alaska: The Alaska Experience*. Atlanta: Gallopede International, 2000.

Schultz, Jeff, and Bill Sherwonit. *Iditarod: The Last Great Race to Nome*. Seattle: Sasquatch Books, 2002.

INDEX

Alaska Highway 10

Anchorage 5, 16, 19, 22, 27

animals 5, 7, 9, 16, 18, 19, 22, 24, 25, 27–28, 29, 31

aurora borealis 29, 31

Benson, Benny 24

borders 12

dog sledders 5, 24, 25, 27

industries 7, 19, 21, 22

   farming 22

   fishing 7, 19, 21, 22

   logging 17, 21

   major businesses 9, 21, 22

   mining 21

Juneau 9, 10, 17

land regions and features 5, 9, 13, 15, 16, 24, 27, 28

   arctic tundra 15

   forests 9

   glaciers 15, 24, 28

   highest point 15

   lakes and rivers 5, 16, 27

   mountains 5, 13, 15

   muskeg 15

Mount McKinley 15, 28

native peoples 6, 13, 19, 21

   Aleuts 6, 13, 19

   American Indians 6

   Eskimos 6, 19, 21

natural resources 9, 10, 17, 21, 22

   gold 9

   oil 10, 17, 21, 22

Nome 5, 9, 25, 27

parks and refuges 17, 22, 27–28

plants 15

population 9, 18–19

   countries represented 19

Russian explorers 6–7

"Seward's Folly" 9

size 13

sports 5, 24, 27

   college teams 27

   Iditarod Race 5, 24, 27

statehood 10

weather and climate 5, 16